I'm Just Here For the FOOD
Cook's Notes

BROUGHT TO YOU BY ALTON BROWN

From the kitchen of

· ·

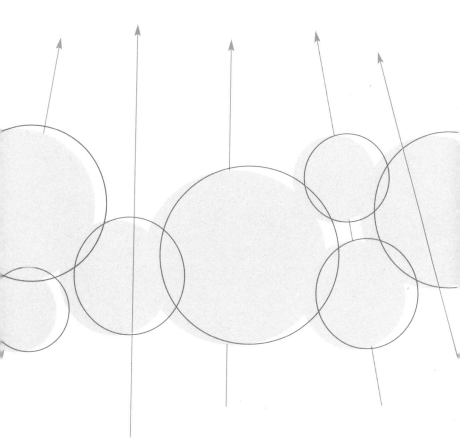

Until I deal with the why, I don't really know the how

Before I had knowledge,
I cooked from recipes

The most underused
tool in the kitchen is
the brain

In the end, a cook must develop his or her own sense of proportion

Remember, flavor is a
noun, taste is a verb

Where there is roast,
there is a gathering

Published in 2003 by

Stewart, Tabori & Chang

A Company of La Martinière Groupe

115 West 18th Street

New York, NY 10011

Export Sales to all countries except Canada, France, and French-speaking Switzerland:

Thames and Hudson Ltd

181A High Holborn

London WC1V 7QX

England

Canadian Distribution:

Canadian Manda Group

One Atlantic Avenue, Suite 105

Toronto, Ontario M6K 3E7

Canada

ISBN: 1-58479-299-X

Project Editor: Marisa Bulzone

Design by Galen Smith and Nancy Leonard

Graphic Production by Kim Tyner

Printed in China by Pimlico

10 9 8 7 6 5 4 3 2 1

First Printing